BRUCE WADE HAS DONE IT!

LAUGH

IN THIS SINGLE BOOK
YOU WILL FIND A NEW REFRESHING
COLLECTION OF GREAT JOKES

IT

GOOD FOR TALKS, PARTIES
AND SPICING UP YOUR LIFE
READ IT AND LAUGH.

UP

V O L U M E 1

LAUGH IT UP!

VOLUME I

By Bruce Wade

Published by:
Acorn, Inc
in conjunction with
F.O.C.U.S. Publishing
12629 N. Tatum Suite 551
Phoenix, AZ 85032

ISBN. . .

Typesetting & Graphics by:
Signal Press, Inc.
7745 East Redfield Rd., Suite 500
Scottsdale, AZ 85308
(602) 991-5156

ABOUT THE AUTHOR

BRUCE WADE lives the good life. Finding humor in the little things of life has been his life long ambition and pursuit. Rarely will you find so many wonderful jokes and stories in one place— brought together by one man who truly knows the value of a good laugh.

These jokes have been tried and tested. They work in many situations. Mr. Wade is a composite of the jokes he so ably shares in his collection.

**"If you can laugh at it
then you can live with it!"**

SMILE!

It takes only 13 muscles;
A frown takes 64.

Preface

"Did you hear about the guy who…?" and everyone's ears perk up. There's a joke coming. Maybe it will be a good one, maybe clever, and just maybe another reason to scorn the joke teller, but whatever, we listen and a few moments are happily spent. We all want to laugh more. A large newspaper did a survey and 51% of Americans said they wanted to do just that - laugh more.

Humor in America is alive and well. It frees up the spirit and helps put the trials of life a little more clearly in focus. Good jokes are hard to come by, though. You can read some joke books from cover to cover and only find a few worth repeating to friends, especially if you want to keep them as friends. Not so from now on because "Super Bruce" is here. I'm on the prowl for the best jokes in America. The research and editing that has gone into this endeavor will continue. We're already compiling the next volume, and we need your help. You'll see pleas for help throughout this book.

Clean jokes are a breed apart. There are enough raunchy joke books on the market that demean people and do no good at all. Whether you need a joke for a family get-together, to prove a point to a teenage son, or for a speech to 2,000 people, I've tried to give you ammunition within this book. Humor teaches because it is lasting. And humor should exist from the beginning of a joke to the ending and not cause offense to the listeners - maybe a little discomfort once in a while, but not offense.

If you have an occasion to speak publicly (and we all do, whether we view it as such or not), then you need to get off your side of the fence and on the side of the audience. We know what we want to say, but who cares? What do they want and need to hear? And how do they want to hear it? Sit out there with them and you'll realize how important a good joke is to prove a point, teach a lesson, change direction, or just to break up the monotony.

If you have a joke to share, send it and if we use it, we'll send you the book free after it is published. In case we receive duplicates of a particular joke, we will honor the first one received.

As you can see, I'm desperate. There are millions of good jokes around but they're hard to find. Maybe by joining forces we can do a better job.

Before I end this preface, let me say thanks to all those who have come before and who now find time to bring smiles to millions. And a special applause to comedians and writers, which for so many years have exemplified how much can be done when good news and information is shared. We're all better because of their efforts and my hope is that individually we can do some good by sharing and caring for others within our reach.

Well, enough of this. It's time for you to get reading and laughing. Here's to you health and wealth, hopefully made better with a little laughter.

Respectfully,

BRUCE WADE

LAUGH IT UP!

A young fellow brought home his bride-to-be to be appraised by his father.

The older man was flabbergasted, chagrined, and embarrassed. He took the boy aside into the next room and whispered in his ear, "I never saw such a homely girl. She's got hair on her chin; her eyes are watching each other; and her teeth are crooked."

"Pop, you don't have to whisper," the son replied. "You can talk louder. She's deaf, too."

....

Fear is taking your kid to a beginning math class and recognizing the person next to him as your tax accountant.

....

A man said after golfing, "What a rotten day! I kept hitting the ball into the water or into the sand. And then my golfing partner, Fred, died on the eighth hole. There I was the rest of the day - hit the ball, drag Fred, hit the ball, drag Fred."

....

Mother: "Howard, get your little sister's hat out of that puddle."

Howard: "I can't, Mom, she's got it strapped too tight under her chin."

....

Rick: "What's the best way to teach a girl to swim?"

Mike: "That requires technique. First you put your left arm around her waist. Then you gently take her left hand and..."

Rick: "She's my sister."

Mike: "Oh, push her off the dock!"

....

An officer in the South Pacific who had been overseas sixteen months received a letter form his wife telling about a prayer their four-year-old daughter made: "Dear Lord, please send me a brother so we will have something to surprise Daddy with when he gets home."

....

It's hard to explain to kids why a nation that spends billions for nuclear bombs is still trying to outlaw firecrackers.

....

Brett sat in Jennifer's parlor and began proposing.

"I'm not a wealthy man," he told her, "but I will be soon. I've got a very rich uncle and I'm his only heir. He's a real old man and so ill that he can't live more than a few months."

A few weeks later Jennifer became Brett's aunt.

....

When my daughter Caroline asked me to baby-sit for her six-month-old identical twins, I was hesitant. "How do I tell April from Stacey?" I asked.

She was busy getting ready to go out. "Just ask Rick," she said, nodding towards her four-year-old, who was engrossed in a cartoon show. "He knows."

Confidently, I undressed the twins and put them in the bath. When I was ready to dress them, I called to Rick. "Which on is which?"

"That's easy," he yelled back, eyes still rivetted on Bugs Bunny. "April always wears blue."

....

Have you heard about the new two-step method to cure yourself of smoking in bed?

(1) Buy a water mattress.

(2) Fill it with gasoline.

....

A surgeon, an architect, and a politician were arguing as to whose profession was the oldest.

Said the surgeon: "Eve was made from Adam's rib, and that surely was a surgical operation."

"Maybe," said the architect, "but prior to that, order was created out of chaos, and that was an architectural job.:

"But ," interrupted the politician, "Somebody created the chaos first!"

....

An elderly Connecticut farmer who had little patience
with children finally surrendered to the charms of his
attractive, young housekeeper, the mother of a ten-year-
old brat.

Soon after the marriage, she went to New York to do
some shopping. Upon her return she asked her son how
he got along with his new father.

"Okay," said the youngster, "every morning he took me
out on the lake in a row boat and let me swim back."

"Heavens, that's a long distance to swim!"

"Oh, I made it all right," said the boy. "Only trouble I
had was getting out of the burlap bag."

. . . .

A very thin man met a very fat man in the hotel lobby.

"From the looks of you," said the fat man, "there might have been a famine."

"Yes," was the reply, "and from the looks of you, you might have caused it."

The decrepit old man drove up to the toll bridge. "Fifty cents," cried the tollman. "Sold," replied the driver.

Here's a suggestion for parents who become naturally worried when their youngsters are away from home, either at camp or college, and neglect to write:

Just send the child your usual letter, then add a postscript something like this: "hope you can use the $20 I am enclosing." Then don't enclose it.

....

Action speaks louder than words but not nearly as of tem.

....

Remember the advice of the Mama Whale to the Baby Whale: Only when you are spouting are you likely to get harpooned!

....

"A horrible thing just happened. I've lost my wallet with five hundred dollars in it. I'll give fifty dollars to anyone who will return it."A voice from the rear: "I'll give one hundred dollars.

Did you hear about the lawyer that believed in reincarnation? In his will he left everything to himself.

....

"My wife should have been a lawyer."
"Why's that?"
"Every time we have an argument and she feels like she's losing, she takes it to a higher court —

"Mommy, what happens to an automobile when it gets too old to run any more?"
"Why, somebody sells it to your dad, for a used car, good as new."

....

An order — and an acknowledgement:
"Send radio — if good, will send check."
"Send check — if good, will send radio."

....

Tax accountant to client: "I've got terrible news for you. Last year was the best year you ever had."

....

....

Two men were up in a hot air balloon and happened to get lost. They spotted a man on the ground and one of them yelled, "Where are we?" The man replied, "You're in a hot air balloon." The man looked at his partner and said, "He's a CPA." "How do you know ?" asked the partner. "Because his information is totally correct and totally worthless."

....

The minister of a church in the financial district closed his sermon with, "Keep in mind: There will be no buying and selling of securities in Heaven!" One parishioner leaned over to another and said, "It doesn't matter. That ain't where the stock market is going."

You can understand why some employees have a hard time analyzing the word BOSS. That's a backward double S.O.B.

You have to be very careful about real estate ads. They use phrases like "a maintenance-free house." A maintenance-free house. That means for the last twenty-five years there hasn't been any maintenance.

....

Timmy had only two pennies in his pocket when he approached the farmer and pointed to a tomato hanging lusciously from a vine.

"Give you two cents for it," the boy offered.

"That kind brings in a nickel," the farmer told him.

"This one?" Timmy asked, pointing to a smaller, greener and less tempting specimen. The farmer nodded agreement.

"Okay," said Timmy, and sealed the deal by placing his two pennies in the farmers hand. "I'll pick it up in about a week."

....

Bosses who hire relatives have a payroll that just won't
QUIT

....

A man needing directions walked up to an Italian carrying two large watermelons, one in each arm. "Which way to the library?" The Italian paused, put down both watermelons, put his hands in the air, and said with a shrug, "I don't know."

....

A ventriloquist is telling Irish jokes in a pub, when an irate Irishman stands up: "You're makin' out we're all dumb and stupid. I outta punch you in the nose."
"I'm sorry sir, I..."
"Not you, " says the Irishman, "I'm talking to that little fella on your knee."

....

How many Californians does it take to water a plant?
Two. One to pour the Perrier and one to massage the leaves.

....

I placed a call to my sister who lives in a small town in Iowa. After I gave the local operator the number she said, "I'll ring now, but I don't think they're home. Their car is gone."

....

I leaned over and whispered in her ear, "I love you terribly." She said, "I know, but we have the rest of our lives to work on it."

....

A man who had been keeping company with a girl for several years took her to a Chinese restaurant. Studying the menu, he asked, "How would you liked your rice – fried or boiled?"

Looking him straight in the eye, she replied, "Thrown."

. . . .

The private eye was giving his client a report on her husband. "I trailed your husband into four bars and then to a bachelor's apartment," he said.

"Aha!" exclaimed the wife. "Go on, go on! What was he doing there?"

"Well, lady," the private eye responded in an embarrassed tone, "Near as I could make out, he was trailing you."

. . . .

The district attorney faced the jury and angrily asked, "In view of all the evidence I presented, what possible excuse can you give for acquitting this man?"

"Insanity, sir," was the foreman's reply.

"What? All twelve of you?"

An American and a Russian were fishing on opposite sides of the river. The American caught fish after fish, while the Russian didn't even get a bite. Finally the Russian yelled across, "Why is it you catch fish and I get none?"

The American thought a minute and then replied, "I guess on your side they are afraid to open their mouths."

Work is what some people have to do if they don't already have jobs with the government.

. . . .

"Waiter, there's a hair in my soup!"

"Is it blonde, sir? We're missing a waitress."

. . . .

Upstairs neighbor: "Didn't you hear me pounding on the floor last night?"

Downstairs neighbor: "Oh, that's all right. We were making a lot of noise ourselves."

. . . .

....

At a rest home two elderly men were trying
to get the attention of two of the ladies, but
they never could seem to get them to look
their way them. So one day the men decided
that to get their attention, they would run
past the ladies sitting in their chairs. They
took off their shirts and ran past them. One
lady said to the other, "What was that?" The
other said, "I don't know, but whatever it was,
it needed ironing."

....

....

Three men were all facing a firing squad.
The men in the squad were loading their
weapons and this gave the men time to talk.
"Listen you two," said the first, "one at a time
we will create a diversion and the one who
creates it will run over that hill over there. I
go first so you can see how it's done."
The squad lined up and the first man yelled,
"Tornado!" As the squad turned to look, he
ran for safety over the hill.
Then the second man yelled as the squad
turned to aim again, "Flash flood!" When the
squad turned around again, he too was gone.
Now it was the third man's turn. As the
squad aimed, he yelled, "Fire!"

....

I'm so depressed. I had to shoot my dog."
"Was he mad?"
"He wasn't exactly pleased."

....

Sally: "What makes your new baby brother cry so
much?"
　Mary: "He doesn't cry so very much. Besides, if all
your teeth were out, your hair gone, and your legs so
weak you couldn't stand on them, I guess you'd feel like
crying too."

....

A synonym is a word you use when you can't spell the
other one.

....

How many firemen does it take to change a light bulb?
　Four. One to change the bulb and three to cut a hole in
the roof.

....

**The definition of an average person is one who
thinks he isn't.**

Then there's the tale of the two story house. The real estate agent told them one story before they bought it and one afterward.

There was a dog at a barber shop that continually stared at the patron getting his hair cut. Finally one man said to the barber: "Your dog likes to watch you cut hair, doesn't he?"

"That isn't it. Sometimes I snip off a bit of ear."

....

When all you have is a hammer, every problem becomes a nail.

....

We were better off when politicians tried to make history, not the eleven o'clock news.

....

Judge: "How could you possibly swindle people who trusted you?"

Prisoner: "But, Judge, people who don't trust you can't be swindled."

....

I just read that last year 6,543,239 people got married . I don't want to start any trouble, but shouldn't that be an even number?

"Aren't people funny?"

"Yes. If you tell a man that there are 270,678,934,341 stars in the universe, he'll believe you – but if a sign says "Fresh Paint," that same man has to make a personal investigation."

....

"Did you give your wife that little lecture on economy you talked about?"

"Yes."

"Any results?"

"Yes – I've got to give up smoking."

....

Believe me, it isn't easy being a camper. You don't know what fear is until you've zipped up your sleeping bag – and the itch on your big toe starts to move!

....

Raising kids is like eating a grapefruit. No matter how you do it, the little squirts get you.

....

．．．．．．．．．．．．．．．．．．．．．．

The Reverend said, "Brother Brown, if you
had two big houses sitting on a hill, would
you give you one to the Church?"
Brother Brown said, "You know, if I had two
houses I'd give one."
"And if you had two Cadillacs would you
give one the the church?"
Again he replied, "You know I'd give you
one of those Cadillacs."
"Brother Brown, if you had two white shirts,
would you give the Church one?"
"Now wait a minute, Reverend, you know I
have two white shirts!"

．．．．．．．．．．．．．．．．．．．．．．

The man was drowning. "Help, I can't swim," he cried, "I can't swim!"

"I can't either," said an old man, sitting on the riverbank fishing. "But I'm not hollerin' about it."

....

How many editors does it take to change a light bulb? Two. One to change the bulb and one to issue a rejection slip to the old bulb.

....

Knock knock.
Who's there?
Anita.
Anita who?
Anita you like I need a hole in the head

....

During the days of the draft a young man received his notice and was told to bring in a urine sample to the Selective Service Headquarters.

Figuring on out-foxing the draft board, the young man filled a bottle with urine from his father, girlfriend, and dog, and then added some of his own. After turning in the sample, he waited for about a half hour.

Finally the lab technician came out. "According to our lab test," he reported, "your father has diabetes, your girlfriend is pregnant, your dog is in heat, and you're in the army."

....

The young man who answered the classified advertisement, "Opportunity of a Lifetime," found himself in the presence of a nervous individual.

"What I am looking for is somebody to do all my worrying," he explained. "Your job will be to shoulder all my cares."

"That's some job. How much do I get?" asked the applicant.

"You get $20,000 to make all my worries your own."

"Where does the $20,000 dollars come from?"

"Ah," said the man, "that is your first worry."

....

You say this fellow is crooked?"

"Is he crooked? Say, he's so crooked even the wool he pulls over your eyes is half cotton."

Two truths: the husband is the head of the household, and the pedestrian has the right of way. Both of them are safe until they try to prove it.

A state trooper heard this plea on his radio: "Does anyone know where I'm at? I'm all screwed up." It was a policeman who had lost his way.

Another voice rang out, bold and authorative: "Would the officer making that last transmission please identify himself?"

After a short silence, a third voice said: "He's not that screwed up."

....

．．．．．．．．．．．．．．．．．．．．．

Two ardent fishermen went on their
vacation and began swapping stories about
different places they had fished, the kind of
tackle used, the best bait, and finally about
some of the fish they had caught.

One of them told of a vicious battle he once
had with a 300-pound salmon. The other
man listened attentively. He frankly admitted
he had never caught anything quite that big.
However, he told about the time his hook
snagged a lantern from the depths of a lake.
The lantern carried a tag saying it was lost
back in 1912. But the strangest thing of all
was the fact that is was a waterproof lantern
and the light was still lit.

For a long time the first man said nothing.
Then he took a deep breath, sighed and
said,"I'll tell you what I'll do," he said slowly.
"I'll take 200 pounds off my fish, if you'll put
out the light in your lantern."

．．．．．．．．．．．．．．．．．．．．．

"George, why don't you play golf anymore?"

"Would you play golf with a fellow who moved the ball with his foot when you weren't watching?" George asked.

"Well, no," admitted the friend.

"Neither will my friends."

....

Two hundred years ago a letter took three days to go from Boston to New York and it was called progress. Today it's called Special Delivery.

....

Bill collector: "Say, I want to collect some back payments on your antique furniture."

Head of the House: "You're crazy. I never bought any antique furniture on the installment plan."

Bill collector: "Well, maybe it wasn't antique when you bought it."

....

A solicitous husband is a person who is interested in his wife's happiness and hires a detective to find out who's responsible for it.

....

The whole idea of summer camp is the buddy system. You do everything with another kid. You walk together, you eat together – for six weeks. It's like a Hollywood marriage, only longer!

....

I'll never forget my honeymoon. My wife put on her sexiest negligee, snuggled up close, and in a very shy voice said, "Dear, now that we're married, can I do anything I want?" I said, "Anything you want." She said "Anything?" I said, "Sure, anything." So she went to sleep.

....

A sign in the gift shop read, "For the man who has everything: a calender to remind him when the payments are due."

....

Little monkeys grow up to be big monkeys; little pigs grow up to be big pigs; but man, wonderful man, can grow up to be either.

....

A wealthy old farmer was having a reunion with his large family and as they all sat down to the table for Sunday dinner, the old man looked around at his six big strapping sons and said:

"I don't see any grandchildren around this table of mine. I want you all to know that I will give $10,000 to the first one of you who presents me with a grandchild. We will now say grace."

When he raised his eyes again, he and his wife were the only ones at the table.

....

....

The happiest people are
those who discover that what
they should be doing and what
they are doing are the same
thing.

....

"Can you name an animal that has eyes and cannot see, legs and cannot walk, but can jump as high as the Empire State Building?"

Everybody racked their brains during a period of deep silence. Finally, they gave up and demanded the solution.

"The answer," he said "is a wooden horse. It has eyes and cannot see and cannot walk."

"Yes," the company agreed. "But how does it jump as tall as the Empire State Building?"

"The Empire State Building," the humorist explained, "cannot jump."

....

Elmo Stink was a country boy who decided to move the big city. Soon after the move he began to notice that people were finding something interesting about his name. So after some consideration he decided to change his name, and filed the necessary legal request. When the court appearance date arrived, Elmo stood before the judge. "Well, young man," said the judge, "I see you want to change your name. What is your name now?"

"Elmo Stink, Your Honor."

"I see," chuckled the judge. "And what would you like to change it to?"

"Aaron Stink, Your Honor. I never did like the name Elmo."

....

What is it when fourteen rabbits in a line are jumping backwards?

A receding hare line.

....

They said the economy is bouncing back. I have news - so are my checks!

Do you ever get the feeling someone is feeding your garden birth control pills?

....

Whenever opportunity knocks, instead of getting off their feet to open the door, most people complain about the noise.

....

The poor man was beside himself. His wife was sick and perhaps dying. He called on the only doctor nearby. "Please, save my wife, doctor! I'll pay anything!"

"But what if I can't cure her?" asked the doctor.

"I'll pay whether you cure her or kill her, if only you'll come right away!"

So the doctor promptly visited the woman, but within a week she died. Soon a bill arrived charging the man a tremendous fee. The tailor couldn't hope to pay, so he asked the local rabbi to arbitrate the case.

"He agreed to pay me for treating his wife," stated the physician, "whether I cured her or killed her."

The rabbi was thoughtful. "Well, did you cure her?" he asked.

"No," admitted the doctor.

"And did you kill her?"

"I certainly did not!" said the physician.

"In that case," the rabbi sad with finality, "you have no grounds on which to base a fee."

> **You know the children have grown up when you find yourself straightening up the house before they come home instead of after.**

The self-made storekeeper had little patience with formal education. When a young man applied for work in his store, the owner said, "Sure I'll give you a job. Sweep up the store."

"But I'm a college graduate," protested the young man.

"Okay, I'll show you how."

....

....

A financial planner was being knocked to
the right and to the left as his cab cruised
down the street at a high speed. When he got
a chance to catch his breath, he finally
complained to the driver.

"You ain't got no cause to worry," said the
cabbie. "I ain't goin' to land back in no
hospital now, after being in one for the last
two years."

Two years, the planner asked, "How awful.
You must have been seriously wounded."

"Nope. Never got a scratch," grinned the
cabbie. "I was a mental case."

....

> **You know you're getting old when you have to put tenderizer on hamburger.**
>
> .

A kind-hearted motorist saw a man struggling to change a tire along side the highway. There was a dirty smear across his face where he had wiped off the sweat with dirty hands. His tie was undone, his shirt collar askew, and obviously he had also wiped his hands on his once-white shirt. Close to him stood a slight woman, immaculately neat, and arguing angrily.

"Look, friend," said the kind-hearted motorist. "I've changed a lot of tires. Is there anything I can do to help?"

"There sure is," replied the man with the tire tool. "My wife is an expert, too. If you will just do all the arguing with her about how this tire ought to be changed, I can concentrate on the dirty work and get the job done."

....

"How did you stop you husband from staying late at the club?"

"When he came in late I called out, 'Is that you Jack,' and my husband's name is Robert."

....

I always bet on those horses that fall apart in the stretch. I bet on one horse that folded so badly, he came in fifth in the race and ninth in the instant replay.

....

If you see two monsters, two werewolves, and two witches in a room together, what should you do?
Hope it's a Halloween party.

Smith puffed heavily on his cigar while loitering in the shopping mall drugstore.

The pharmacist had to speak forcefully to him. "Please, sir, there's no smoking."

"But I bought the cigar here."

"Look," pleaded the druggist, "we also sell laxatives here, but you can't enjoy them on the premises."

....

On her son's seventeenth birthday a mother pleadingly asked, "Promise me you'll tell me when you start smoking. Don't let me find it out from the neighbors."

"Don't worry about me, Mom," the son replied. "I qut smoking a year ago."

....

Mrs. Heckstein was preparing dinner when a beggar came to her door. "Lady, I haven't eaten for three days. Have you got something for me?

"I haven't got much," said Mrs. Heckstein.

"Would you like some soup left from the night before?"

"That would be great!"

"Good, then you can come back tomorrow."

....

Mom: "I'm so glad to see you sitting so quietly while your father naps."

Son: "I'm watching his cigarette burn down to his fingers."

....

Waiting to borrow some money to make a six-month tour of Europe, a man went to the bank where he had done business for years. The bank refused the loan.

He went to another bank and obtained the loan without any difficulty. Then he bought a five-pound fish, had it wrapped, and put it in his safe-deposit box at the first bank as he joyfully left town for six months.

....

A reporter, interviewing a man who had reached his 99th birthday, said, "I certainly hope I can come back next year and see you reach 100."

"Can't see why not, young feller," the old-timer replied, "You look healthy enough to me."

....

A group of American tourists were being guided through an ancient castle in Europe.

"This place," the guide told them, "is 600 years old. Not a stone in it has been touched, nothing altered, nothing replaced in all those years."

"Well," said one woman dryly, "they must have the same landlord I have."

....

"Do you believe in life after death?" an employer asked the office boy.

"Oh yes sir," was the reply.

" Ah, then everything is in order, because after you had gone to you grandfather's funeral yesterday, he came here to see you."

....

Hardy was on trial for armed robbery. The jury came out and the foreman announced, "Not guilty."

"Wonderful," shouted Hardy. "Does that mean I can keep the money?"

....

"It's an outrage the way those nudist are carrying on in that apartment," the old woman told the policeman when he answered the call. "I'm ashamed."

The cop looked out the window and could see nothing but a vast courtyard, a road, and an apartment building in the distance. "I can't see a thing," he shrugged,

"Of course you can," the old lady replied. "But just have a look through these binoculars and you'll see plenty."

....

....

Television is the device that
brings into your living room people
who you'd never invite into your
home in person.

....

An attorney claimed that his dog, when given money, would go to the newsstand and buy a paper. His friend insisted on a demonstration and handed the dog some money. The dog trotted off, but an hour later he had still not returned with the paper.

"How much did you give him?" asked the owner.

"Five dollars."

"Well, that explains it. When you give him five dollars he goes to the movies."

....

A lot of people are desperate today. A fellow walked up to me and said, "You see a cop around here?" I said no. He said, "Stick 'em up!"

....

A friend of mine was complaining that the new house he had rented had grass growing through the living room floor.

I asked, "How much rent are you paying?"

He said, "$500 a month."

I said, "What do you expect for $500 a month - broccoli?"

....

A mother took her little boy to a psychiatrist and asked, "Can a boy ten years old marry a beautiful star like Liz Taylor?"

The psychiatrist said, "Of course not, it's impossible."

The mother said to the kid, "See, what did I tell you. Now go and get a divorce."

....

Bill: "I'm beggining to think my attorney just wants to see how much he can get out of me."

Jim: "Why's that?"

Bill: "He charged me $25 for waking up at night thinking my case."

Prices are just ridiculous. Yesterday I went into one of those fried chicken places and spent $1.50 for a wing and a drumstick. It's the first time I ever paid an arm and a leg for an arm and a leg!

....

"You look sad, my friend. What are you thinking about?"

"My future."

"What makes it seem so bad?"

"My past."

....

If George Washington was so honest what's his picture doing on a dollar bill that's only worth 37¢?

....

The lonely stranger entered a restaurant in New York.

"May I take your order?" the waitress inquired.

"Yes," he replied. "Two eggs and a kind word."

The waitress brought the eggs and was leaving when the man asked her, "What about the kind word?"

She leaned over and said, "Don't eat the eggs."

....

Bill Collector: "Say, I want to collect some back payments on your antique furniture."

Head of the House: "You're crazy. I never bought any antique furniture on the installment plan.

Bill Collector: "Well, maybe it wasn't antique when you bought it."

....

A new tenor makes his debut at the Met. He sings an aria and the applause is so overwhelming that he sings it again. They try to go on with the opera but the applause won't stop, so he is brought forward to sing it again. This goes on until he has sung it eight times. Finally he steps forward and addresses his audience:

"My, friends, this is too much. The honor you have bestowed on me is overwhelming and no matter what becomes of me in the future, this will have been my greatest operatic moment. However, the opera must go on and my voice is tiring, so please don't ask me to sing it again."

Voice from the balcony: "You'll sing it till you get it right!"

I'm a little depressed today. I've been paying into a plan that allows me to retire at fifty-five on twelve hundred a month. I just found out that means calories.

I wouldn't belong to any club that would have me as a member.

....

Last month my wife decided to save money on electricity. We didn't turn on any lights; we didn't watch TV; we didn't play the radio; we even unplugged the refrigerator. The electric bill for thirty-one days was eight cents. It would have been zero, but the electric company kept ringing the bell to find out what was wrong!

....

Mrs. Smith: "The post office is very careless sometimes, don't you think?"

Mrs. Jones: "Yes, dear, why?"

Mrs. Smith: "My husband sent me a postcard yesterday from Philadelphia, where he is staying on business, and the silly post office people put an Atlantic City mark in the envelope."

I was reporting for the graveyard shift as a supply clerk in a factory when the clerk from the previous shift pointed out a small box that had been left on the loading dock. Printed on all sides of the box was the warning: "Danger! Do Not Touch!" The clerk had already called the plant supervisor for advice and was told to stay clear of the box until management could analyze the situation the next day.

I wouldn't even breathe on the ominous-looking package until the supply foreman arrived in the morning. After removing gloves and safety glasses, he carefully opened the box. Inside were 25 signs that read: "Danger! Do Not Touch!"

A doctor was consulted by a prizefighter who was troubled with insomnia.

"Have you tried counting sheep?" asked the doctor.

"Yes, but it doesn't help. Every time I get up to nine, I jump up."

....

Did you ever get the feeling that if they put a space on the ballot labeled NONE OF THE ABOVE it would get 92 percent of the vote?

There were two guys hiking in the woods and they came across a bear. One of them bent down and started taking off his hiking boots and putting on his tennis shoes. The other one said, "Hey, that's not going to do you any good-putting on your tennis shoes. You're not going to outrun the bear." He said, "All I've got to do is outrun you."

....

The sad and sorrowful young man approached his sweetheart. She watched him with anxious eyes, and asked:

"How did Father take it?"

"All right," he replied.

"I'm so glad!" she cried.

"Well, I can't say I am. At first he wouldn't listen to me."

"Did you tell him that you had five thousand dollars saved and in the bank?"

"Yes, after all else failed."

"And what did Father do then?"

"Do!" replied the young man. "He borrowed it!"

．．．．．．．．．．．．．．．．．．．．．．．

My son flunked history. I said,
"History! When I was your age, that was
my easiest subject!" He said, "Big deal.
When you were my age, what had
happened?"

．．．．．．．．．．．．．．．．．．．．．．．

One day, after my kindergarten class sang "The Old Gray Mare," I asked, "What is an old gray mare?" One little boy piped up, "He's the guy that runs the city."

....

"There are advantages and disadvantages about this property," said the honest real estate agent. "To the north is the gas works, to the east a glue factory, to the south a fish and chip shop, and to the west a sewage farm. Those are the disadvantages."

"What are the advantages?" asked the prospective buyer.

The agent replied, "You can always tell which way the wind is blowing,"

....

Nowadays there's no such thing as a kid getting left back. Mark my words, ten years from now the dumbest kid on the block will come home and say, "I just got a fud." His parents will ask, "What's a fud?" He'll say, "I dunno, it just says fud - Ph.D."

He crossed a Mexican jumping bean with pancake batter and got self-flapping pancakes.

....

44

People wonder how rock groups can afford all those expensive microphones and amplifiers and tuners and instruments. Then again, look how much money they save on music lessons.

Do you ever get the feeling that you're going nowhere-- and have already arrived.

....

The Internal Revenue Service has streamlined it's tax form for this year. It goes like this:
  (A) How much did you make last year?
  (B) how much have you left?
  (C) Send B.

....

A guy walked up to me and said, "Stick 'em down."
I said, "You mean stick 'em up."
He said, "No wonder I haven't made any money."

....

An atheist is a person who has no invisible means of support.

....

This restaurant is so exclusive, if you want water, they ask you, "What year?"

....

Recessions take a toll on everyone. A drug store in a small town was closed down by its creditors. As the saddened proprietor left the premises for the last time, he paused long enough to tack his sign on the front door:
"Our doors are locked. The following services, formerly available here, may be had elsewhere from now on: Ice-water at a fountain in the park. General information from the policeman at the corner. Change of dollar at the bank. Matches and scratch pads at the hotel. Magazines for browsing from the doctor. Bus information at the terminals. And loafing at any other location of your own choosing."

Personally, I don't mind paying twenty-nine cents to mail a letter. To show what a sport I am, I'd even be willing to donate five bucks to the parcel post department - so they can buy a dictionary and look up the meaning of the word "fragile."

....

A tourist stopped his car on the road and asked a country boy how far it was to Titusville.

The boy replied: "It's 24,999 miles the way you're goin', but if you turn around it's about four miles."

....

I owe a lot to smoking. thanks to smoking, I now puff on cigarettes, cigars, pipes and stairs.

This will be a rather short talk tonight and you can thank three people for it: my partner, who took a forty-five minute speech and edited it down to thirty minutes; my wife, who took the thirty-minute speech and edited it down to fifteen minutes; and my secretary, who took the fifteen-minute speech and lost it.

....

....

A young mother was worried about her nine-year-old son. No matter how much she scolded, he kept running around with his shirt tails flapping. On the other hand, her neighbor had four boys, and each of them always wore his shirt neatly tucked in. Finally, in desperation the young mother asked her neighbor to tell her the secret.

"Oh, it's all very simple," she replied. "I just take all their shirts and sew an edging of lace on the bottom."

....

A mosquito is a small insect designed by God to make us feel better about flies.

....

A woman was showing a contractor through the second floor of her new house, advising him what colors to paint the rooms. "I'd like the bedroom done in blue," she instructed.

The contractor walked over to the window and shouted, "Green side up! Green side up!"

"I want the bathroom in white," continues the woman.

Again the contractor yelled out the window, "Green side up! Green side up!"

"The halls should be done in gray!"

Again the contractor shouted out the window, "Green side up! Green side up!"

"Every time I give you a color, you shout 'Green side up!'" the woman snapped angrily.

"I'm sorry , ma'am," the contractor explained. "But I've got three dumb laborers down there putting in the lawn."

....

> **Dear Sir: What would go well with the red, green, and yellow socks my wife gave me for Christmas?**
> **Answer: Hip boots.**

A little boy was saying his go-to-bed prayers in a very low voice.

"I can't hear you, dear," his mother whispered.

"Wasn't talking to you," said the small one firmly.

....

He was so rich he had Swiss money in an American bank.

....

Am I wrong? I thought we had a deal with the Post Office. We were going to show a little code and they were going to show a little zip!

....

A tourist was visiting Arizona. While gazing at the artifacts that were everywhere, he met an old Indian who acted as an unofficial guide.

"How old are these vases?" asked the tourist.

"Exactly one hundred million and three years old," was the Indian's reply.

"How can you be so definite?" inquired the tourist.

"Oh, a geologist told me they were one hundred million years old," replied the Indian, "and that was exactly three years ago."

....

There was an attorney, a banker, and a CPA who were in a boat together. They were way out in the water and had lost their oars. They decided that one of them should swim back to shore to get help. There was just one catch, the boat was surrounded by sharks. The CPA volunteered to go, but the attorney said, "No, let me go." So he jumped into the water. Immediately, the sharks moved aside and gave him a clear path to shore. The CPA said, "My goodness, I've seen a miracle." "No," replied the banker, "that's just a **professional courtesy**."

Success and Failure. We think of them as opposites, but they're really not. They're companions - the hero and the sidekick.

....

Have you ever been to one of those swingin' retirement communities? It's really something. First time I ever saw anybody mainline Ben-Gay!

....

Teacher: "Renaldo, if you put your hand in one pants' pocket and you find 30 cents, and you put your hand in the other pants' pocket and you find 70 cents, what would you have?"
Renaldo: "I'd have on somebody else's pants!"

....

"If God had believed in permissiveness, he would have given us the Ten Suggestions"

They say the average taxpayer works four months out of every year for the government - which is very disturbing. I'm not even sure people who work for the government work four months out of every year for the government.

....

America is a land where most citizens vote for Democrats, but hope to live like Republicans.

....

I heard a joke a few years ago about a tenant sharing the unit with two other tenants. He finally went to the authorities complaining that Bill had 12 dogs and never let them outside. The place just stunk of dogs. And George had nine cats and he also kept them in. He wanted relief because he couldn't stand the smell or the mess. The official questioned, "Why don't you open the window for some fresh air?" He replied, "What, and let all my pigeons out?"

....

My wife is not talking to me since I patched a tire with one of her pancakes.

....

The policeman stopped a man going down the street clad in a barrel.

"Are you a poker player?" he asked.

"No," the man replied, "but I just left some fellows who are."

....

A true sports fan is one who can leave the game and ask, "What cheerleaders?"

For those of you who are making out your income tax, remember that birth control pills are deductible - but only if they don't work.

....

....

There was a lady selling pretzels down at a New York subway for 50¢. Every day a nice looking gentleman walked by and dropped in 50¢ and walked on without taking a pretzel. He did this day after day. One day she chased after him and said, "Mister, mister!" He turned around and said, "I know, you want to know why I put in 50¢ every day and walk on without taking a pretzel." She said, "No, mister. I just wanted to tell you that tomorrow the price goes up to 75¢."

....

A farmer owned two horses. He had trouble telling them apart, so he cut one horse's tail very short. That didn't work, though, because the tail grew right back. Next, he trimmed one horse's mane. That didn't work either because it too soon grew back. Finally, he measured both horses. He found out that the gray horse was two inches taller than the black horse.

. . . .

"Do you know that when I go to heaven I'm going to tell Bill Shakespeare that I don't believe he wrote all those plays."
"Ah, but suppose he doesn't happen to be in heaven?"
"In that case, you can tell him."

. . . .

Our son has been gone to camp for two weeks and all we've received from him is one letter. He wants to know if fingers can be transplanted.

One new stock broker had a car he had to keep moving. The minute he stopped people thought it was an accident.

....

Lillian Carter finally give in to an interview. All went will for a while, but the interviewer finally became indignant when talking about honesty.

"What do you feel abut your son, the President, telling small fibs--and just what is you definition of a small lie?"

Miss Lillian paused and thought, then said, "Well, do you remember when you first came in and I told you how nice you looked...."

....

Her mouth is so big her dentist can use both hands.

....

The university I attended has several stray dogs that live on campus. One day, a rather motley-looking hound ambled into a large lecture hall and proceeded to bark loudly at the professor. After vainly trying to talk over the racket, the professor gave up. Turning to the dog, he said, "If you're going to stay for this lecture, you'll have to behave and act like the rest of the students."

To the delight of the class, the dog curled up on the floor and went to sleep.

I bought my wife a cookbook but she couldn't use it. Every recipe started with "Take a Clean."

I have a problem with my car. The engine won't start and the payments won't stop.

Jaun walked into class about 40 minutes late. "You should have been here at nine o'clock," said the teacher. "Why? What happened?" asked the boy.

....

"I'd like a pair of stockings for my wife."
"Sheer?"
"No she's at home."

....

"Is Ink so very expensive, Father?"
"Why, no, what makes you think so?"
"Well, mother seems quite disturbed because I spilled some on the hall carpet.

....

She's
on
the 110th
day
of a
10-day
beauty
plan.

....

Benson stopped at Finelli's Fish Market on his way home from fishing all day.

"Throw me five red snappers," he said to Finelli.

"Why should I throw them?" asked the shopkeeper.

"I want to be able to say I caught them ."

....

The tribe had eaten the missionary and had thoroughly enjoyed him. Next day one of the cannibals, poking about the dead man's belongings, found a magazine. He began tearing out pictures of men and women, and children, cramming them into his mouth and chewing them.

The chief watched him for a while and then asked, "Say, is that dehydrated stuff any good?"

....

Old age is when the only thing you can really sink your teeth into is water.

....

A famed explorer was captured by savages in the wild of Africa. They were dancing around him in preparation for the kill when an idea struck the explorer--he would awe them with "magic." From his pocket he took a cigarette lighter.

"See," he said, "I am a fire-maker!" And with a flick of his thumb, the lighter burst into flame. The savages fell back in astonishment.

"Magic!" cried the explorer in triumph.

"Sure is," replied the chief. "Only time we ever saw a lighter work for the first time."

....

Trying to sell his new and totally omniscient computer to the youthful businessman, the salesman invited his skeptical client to ask it a question--any question. The executive sat down and typed out his query: "Where is my father?" The machine rapidly printed the reply: "Your father is fishing in Michigan." "This contraption doesn't know what it's talking about," bellowed the prospective customer. "My father's been dead for twenty years."

Certain that his creation was infallible, the salesman suggested, "Why don't you ask the same question in a different form."

The chap then confidently typed: "Where is my mother's husband?" To which the mechanical brain answered: "Your mother's husband has been dead for twenty years. Your father has just landed and three-pound trout."

....

Her mouth is so big she can eat a banana sideways.

....

61

They have a new thing nowadays called Nicotine Anonymous. It's for people who want to stop smoking. When you feel a craving for a cigarette, you simply call up another member and he comes over and you get drunk together.

....

A traveling salesman arrives in a country store where he finds four men playing poker with a fox terrier. He becomes more amazed when he watches the dog call for two cards, raise his bet and rake in the pot.

Finally he says, "That's amazing. I've never seen such a smart dog."

"He ain't smart," says one of the men at the table. Whenever he gets a real good hand he wags his tail."

....

A hotel is a place where people often give up good dollars for poor quarters.

....

"Mister, I haven't tasted food in a week."
"Don't worry, it still tastes the same to me."

I think the Internal Revenue Service deserves a lot of credit.

It's brought poverty within reach of us all!

....

....

I had to buy my teen-age
daughter a car. It was the
only way I could get to
use the phone.

....

When the Tennessee tackle finally handed in his homework, the instructor read it and then wrote down "O."

"I really don't think I deserve a zero," complained the lineman.

"I don't either," agreed the instructor, "but it's the lowest grade I'm permitted to give."

....

The only time most men can keep their wives guessing is when they're dancing with them.

....

Dr. Lamb had just completed the operation and was washing up. He was joined by one of the young interns, who inquired, "How did Mrs. Fuller's appendectomy go?"

"Appendectomy?" shrieked the surgeon. "I thought it was an autopsy!"

....

What do you get when you cross a centipede and a turkey?

Drumsticks for everyone.

....

Q: How old would a person be who was born in 1940?

A: Man or woman?"

....

Three turtles decided they would go for a picnic down by the banks of the river. They packed their lunches and arrived at the river. Before they could begin eating, it started to rain. They decided one must go back after an umbrella so they could eat in a dry area. The smallest turtle was the one who finally agreed to go if the others would promise not to eat the sandwiches while he was gone. It was agreed.

They waited an hour, a day, a week, until finally a month had gone by. Still the turtle did not return…Finally, one turtle said to the other, "He's not coming back, let's go ahead and eat the sandwiches." Just then the little turtle stuck his head out from behind the nearby rock and said, "If you do, I won't go."

....

Thomas Edison said that genius is one percent inspiration and ninety-nine percent perspiration. I hate to think of anyone that sweaty handling electricity.

....

A single CPA who was a stranger in town was taken to a dance at a deaf and dumb hospital by a doctor friend of his.

"But how on earth can I ask a deaf and dumb girl to dance?" he asked.

"Just smile and bow to her," explained the doctor, who had done it before.

So the young man picked out a pretty girl, smiled and bowed to her, and away they danced. They danced not only one dance but three, and he was on the point of asking her for another dance when a strange man approached her and said, "Darling, when are we doing to have another dance? It's been over an hour since I danced with you."

"I don't know, dear," said the girl tenderly. "I don't know how to get away from this deaf and dumb guy!"

....

My husband and I received an invitation to a party at the home of the president of the college. The invitation read: "Semi-Formal." Calling to accept, I asked the president's secretary if that meant I should wear a long dress or a short dinner dress with high heels.

"Don't worry about it," she replied. "We just put in 'semi-formal' so the students will wear shoes."

....

How many college basketball players does it take to change a light bulb?
Only one, but he gets three credits for doing it.

I never realized how much work a garden is. You show me any garden - if the flowers look like heaven - the gardener looks like the other place!

....

The ironies of life: If you own a dog in a big city and go out for a walk, he protects you from the muggers who would never see you if you didn't have to take the dog out for a walk!

....

Son: "Pop, I got into trouble at school today and it's all your fault."
Dad: "How's that?"
Son: "Remember, I asked you how much $500,000 was?"
Dad: "Yes, I remember."
Son: "Well, 'a helluva lot" isn't the right answer."

....

In Congress, after all is said and done - more is said than done.

....

> **The first sign of old age is when you hear "Snap, crackle, and pop" in the morning and it isn't your cereal.**

Did you hear the one about Pedro, the bank robber? He went into town and stole all of the money from the bank. The sheriff was so mad he got up a posse to track Pedro down. Only there was one problem. He didn't speak Spanish. So he hired Jose to go with him. They finally tracked Pedro down up in the mountains. Then the sheriff said "Jose, go over there and tell Pedro I want the money back." So Jose said, "Pedro, the sheriff is really mad, man, he wants the money back." Pedro said "Well, I'm not going to tell him where it is, I hid it." Jose says to the sheriff, "Sheriff, Pedro says he's not going to tell where the money is, he hid it." The sheriff says, "You go back over there and tell him to tell me where he hid it."

"Pedro, he wants you to tell him where you hid the money."

"Well, I'm not going to tell him."

Jose goes back to the sheriff and says, "Pedro says he's not going to tell you."

So the sheriff says, "Jose, you go over to Pedro and tell him if he doesn't tell me where the money is, I'll blow his head off."

So Jose goes over to Pedro and says, "Pedro, Sheriff says if you don't tell him, he'll blow your head off."

Pedro says, "Ok, ok. Next to the bank there is a church, behind the church is a well. I hid the money down in the well."

Jose turns to the sheriff and says, "Sheriff, Pedro says to go ahead and blow his head off!"

Before a huge banquet: Tonight I want you all to forget problems, relax, and enjoy yourself. After all, isn't it ridiculous how little it takes to upset people? Right now I could say two words that would ruin the evening for every waiter in this room: "Separate checks."

....

Am I wrong? I thought we had a deal with the Post Office. We were going to show a little code and they were going to show a little zip!

....

They say that kids today don't know what hard work means. They certainly do. That's why so many of them are on welfare.

Two boys went to a pizza parlor. The waitress asked if they were ready to order. They ordered a medium pizza with pepperoni and cheese. The waitress asked if they wanted it cut into six or eight pieces. One of the boys said, "Six, I'm not hungry enough to eat eight pieces."

....

I had a friend who was investing in gold. He said, "Yes, investing in gold has made me a millionaire. I used to be a multi-millionaire."

....

Diplomacy is the art of letting someone else get in your way.

....

"I don't think I look thirty-five, do you?" a wife asked her husband.

"No, I don't," he said. "But you used to."

....

Sign on a Greek tailor's shop:
   Euripides
   Wefixades

....

The president of the congregation had to undergo surgery. The board met to decide how to show their concern. Finally, it was agreed that the secretary of the congregation would visit the president in the hospital.

Two days after the operation, the secretary visited the sickroom. "I bring you the good wishes of our board," he said. "We hope you get well and live to be 120!"

The president smiled back weakly.

"And that was an official resolution," continued the secretary, "passed by a vote of twelve to nine."

....

I just figured out why there are so many problems in the business world: Any woman smart enough to be a secretary is too smart to be a secretary!

....

MacGregor had a toothache and went to Dr. Fry.

"What do you charge for extracting a tooth?" asked the Scotsman.

"Fifty dollars," replied the dentist.

"Fifty dollars for only twenty seconds' work?" exclaimed MacGregor.

"Well," replied the dentist, "if you want, I could extract it very slowly."

....

Did you ever feel that your sales staff couldn't sell pickles in a maternity ward?

....

．．．．．．．．．．．．．．．．．．．．

At a large party a Hollywood hostess
decided to sing. In an off-pitch voice she
rendered "Carry Me Back to Old Virginia."
She really belted the song, and as she sang
she noticed a distinguished, white-haired
guest bow his head and weep quietly. When
she finished, the hostess approached the old
man and said, "Pardon me, sir, but are you a
Virginian?"

"No, ma'am," said the elderly guest,
wiping away a tear. "I'm a musician."

．．．．．．．．．．．．．．．．．．．．

Fear is taking your kid to a beginning math class and recognizing the person next to him as your tax accountant.

....

I'm reminded of a woman who calls her attorney. She wants a divorce.
He asks, "Do you have any grounds?"
"Yes, we have a lovely acre."
"No, I mean, do you have a grudge?"
"No, but we have a carport."
"That's not what I mean! Does he beat you up or something?"
"No, I get up before my husband every morning."
"Come on lady, just tell me why you want a divorce."
"Because I just can't carry on a decent conversation with that man."

I'll tell you how money hungry this hospital is. When have you ever heard of pay bedpans?

....

The other day I walked into a place to buy a suit...I told the salesman I'd like to see something cheap...He told me to look in the mirror.

....

About a year after her husband died, the widow herself died. When she arrived at the pearly gates she asked if she might see her former husband.

"What's his name?"

"Fred Smith."

"You'll have to give us a better identification. How about his last words? We classify new arrivals that way."

"Well," she replied, "just before he died Fred said, "Kate, if you ever waste any of my hard-earned money, I'll turn over in my grave."

"Oh, sure. We know him. We call him Whirling Fred up here."

....

Legend has it that Columbus stepped onto the soil of the New World, dug a hole, and planted a sprig of mistletoe. Then he told the Indians to kiss their country good-bye.

....

I've got nothing against taxes. It's just that every time my ship comes in, the government unloads it.

> The sergeant looked disdainfully at the new recruits. "Men," he shouted, "I have a job for the laziest rookie here. Will the laziest man step forward?"
>
> Instantly, all the men stepped forward - all but one,
>
> "Why don't you step up to the front with the others?" demanded the sergeant.
>
> "Too much trouble," drawled the rookie.

No
man knows
less than
the the
man who
knows all.

The coach of a Little League team called one of his players over to him and said he would like to explain some of the principles of sportsmanship.

"We don't believe in temper tantrums, screaming at the umpires, using bad language, or sulking when we lose. Do you understand what I am saying?"

The boy nodded.

"All right, then," said the coach, "do you think you can explain it to your father jumping around over there in the stands?"

Once upon a time, a mean, old mountaineer fell sick and died. There were no funeral directors back in the hills then, and embalming was not yet practiced. So the widow and the family dressed the body and placed it in the coffin. As the deceased was being carried from the house, one pallbearer stumbled, causing the coffin to crash into a gatepost. The knock somehow revived the old mountaineer, who sat up yelling at everyone-in sight.

The man lived for over a year and was as mean as ever. Then he got sick and died again. Once more the body was put in the coffin and the pallbearers lifted their burden. As they shuffled by, the long-suffering widow lifted her head and said, "Watch out for that gatepost!"

....

It's revolutionary Paris, 1789, and three spies from England are about to be guillotined.

"Do you want to be beheaded on your back or your front?" the executioner asked Smith. "On my back," said Smith. "I'm not afraid of death."

So Smith was laid back under the knife. The executioner pulled the lever. Thud...and the knife jammed. Smith was reprieved because no man can be sentenced to death twice.

Hoskins was next. He too chose to face the knife. Again the blade jammed, and Hoskins was reprieved. Murphy was third. "Back or front?"

"If it's good enough for Smith and Hoskins, it's good enough for me," and so Murphy was laid on his back under the blade.

"Wait a minute," he said. "I think I can see why it jams."

....

What is happening to this world? This morning I dialed a number and said, "I'd like to talk to Mitchell R. Parker, dean of the Perfect Diction Institute." A voice said, "Thpeaking!"

Driving across campus, I noticed a young man on a bicycle. His T-shirt announced his future occupation: "I am going to be a doctor." The sign on the back of his bicycle read: "I am going to be a Mercedes."

....

A young married couple spending a week at a famous spa had nothing but bad luck, and on the sixth day were down to there last two dollars and a ticket to the local race track.

"Let me go out there alone today," said the young man. "I've got a hunch."

He picked a 40-to-one shot in the first race and won. Every succeeding race was won by a long shot on which he had bet. At the end of the day he had amassed more than ten thousand dollars.

On his way back to the hotel, he stopped off at one of the gambling casinos to cash in further on his good luck. Within an hour he head run his bankroll up to a neat 40 thousand dollars at roulette. On the point of leaving, he had a new hunch and the entire 40 thousand went on black.

The ball bounced, rolled, and settled. The croupier called "Red!"

The young man made his way back to his hotel room, sat down, and lit a cigarette. His wife asked, "How did you make out?"

"I lost two dollars," he nonchalantly replied.

....

Lincoln called in Bed Vade and Senator Daniel Voorhees to discuss the appointment of an Indian commissioner, explaining what kind of man he wanted to appoint.

"Gentlemen, for an Indian commissioner," said the President, "I want a pure-minded, moral, Christian man - frugal and self-sacrificing."

"I think," interrupted Voorhees, "that you won't find him."

"Why not?"

"Because, Mr. President, he was crucified about two thousand years ago," said the senator.

If Patrick Henry thought taxation without representation was bad, he should see it with representation!

....

To increase circulation, a certain newspaper advertised an accident policy free to all new subscribers. A few days later, this advertisement appeared in the paper: "L.M. Collier subscribed to our paper and was given a free accident policy. On his way home from work, he fell down a flight of stairs and broke an arm, a jaw, and both legs. The accident policy paid him $1,000. You may be the lucky one tomorrow."

....

> **Football is a game in which twenty-two big, strong, healthy fellas run around like crazy for three hours - while fifty thousand people who really need the exercise watch them.**

Even my own bank doesn't have confidence in me. I have the only checks in town with three things printed on them - my name, address, and "INSUFFICIENT FUNDS."

....

Mrs. Brown was aging. She had passed 81 and was having some "woman trouble." Upon the advice of her daughter, she went to visit a gynecologist. She remained quiet throughout the examination, but when it was over she turned to Dr. Roberts.

"Dr. Roberts," she said, "you seem to be such a nice young man. Tell me, does your mother know how you're making a living?"

....

All candidates have one thing in common: They promise us a rose garden, but they deliver only the fertilizer.

....

The big problem in restaurants in tipping. Tipping is like prunes. You always have to ask yourself, "Is one enough? Is five too many?"

....

Frogs have it easy.
They can eat what bugs them.

....

I know a salesman who could have sold bagels to the PLO.

....

You would have loved this town. If is wasn't for bowling, there wouldn't have been any culture at all.

....

Only lawyers write documents longer than 5,000 words and call them briefs.

....

A boss is like the center on a football team. He always feels things are going on behind his back.

....

APPENDIX
A

Some times a few words can teach a powerful lesson. The following are some great axioms to live by.

Bruce

The road to success is always under construction.

....

Life is not so much a matter of position as of dispostion.

....

The best vitamin for making friends, B-1.

....

He who throws mud, loses ground.

....

A pint of example is worth a gallon of advice.

....

"If you don't care where you're going, any road will get you there."

He who throws mud, loses ground.

....

Nobody raises his own reputation by lowering others.

....

Nothing ruins the truth like stretching it.

....

Dieters - people that are thick and tired of it.

....

Ideas won't work unless you do.

....

The future is purchased by the present.
....

One thing you can't recycle is wasted time.
....

Lost time is never found again.
....

A hard thing about business is minding your own.
....

He who forgives ends the quarrel
....

"A smile is an inexpensive way to improve your looks."

"Triumph is just 'umph' added to try."

If the going gets easy, you may be going downhill.

....

Jumping to conclusions can be a bad exercise.

....

A turtle makes progress when it sticks it's neck out.

....

Failure is the path of least persistence.

....

Hard work is the yeast that raises the dough.

....

99

Patience is counting down without blasting off.

....

God's last name is not "Dammit."

....

Some folks won't look up until they are flat on their backs.

....

Children need more models than critics.

....

If you want your dreams to come true, don't oversleep.

....

"A ship is safe in the harbor, but that's not what ships are for."

"The tide in every man's life rises every so often, and when it does, its not time to wax the surf board."

Friend - One who knows all about you and likes you just the same.

....

Money talks and often just says, "Good-bye."

....

Birds have bills too, but they keep on singing.

....

Forbidden fruit is responsible for many a bad jam.

....

A good example is the best sermon.

....

99

The Ten Commandments are not multiple choice.

....

Minds are like parachutes - they function only when open.

....

Live as you wish your kids would.

....

People don't fail, they give up.

....

When looking for faults use a mirror, not a telescope.

....

"The biggest fish you'll ever catch is still swimming in the ocean."

Old Irish Proverb

"Too many of us speak twice before we think."

Kindness, a language deaf people can hear and blind can see.

....

Heaviest thing to carry - a grudge.

....

A smooth sea never made a skillful sailor.

....

A small leak can sink a great ship.

....

You can't direct the wind, but you can adjust your sails.

....

"

66

We lie loudest when we lie to ourselves.

....

Tact is the ability to see others as they wish to be seen

....

One thing you can give and still keep - your word.

....

A friend walks in when everyone else walks out.

....

If you must cry over spilt milk then please try to condense it.

....

99

> "A quitter never wins - A winner never quits."

"Success comes in cans. Failure comes in can'ts."

Behavior is the mirror in which everyone shows thier image.

"

....

Make friends before you need them.

....

It's not the load that breaks you down, it's the way you carry it.

....

The smallest good deed is better than the grandest intention.

....

The greatest of all faults is to imagine you have none.

....

Want to earn a few extra bucks for your youth group or favorite charity? Buy and sell this book in volume. Get wholesale prices and resell for a profit. What a fine way to earn a little extra and help people enjoy life a little more--all at the same time.

Suggested retal price is $7.95

Quanity	Your Cost	You Make
Under 50	$6.00	$1.95
50-100	5.50	2.45
Over 100	5.00	2.95

Send your order with checks or money order to:
ACORN, Inc.
12629 N. Tatum
Suite #551
Phoenix, AZ 85032

Please include $5.00 shipping & handling for each grouping of 25 books.